Subject Matter of the Artist:

Writings by Robert Goodnough, 1950–1965

Subject Matter of the Artist:
Writings by Robert Goodnough, 1950–1965

Edited by Helen A. Harrison | Foreword by Irving Sandler

SOBERSCOVE PRESS
CHICAGO

SOBERSCOVE PRESS
1926 West Erie Street
Chicago, IL 60622 USA
www.soberscovepress.com

Library of Congress Control Number: 2013935548
ISBN-13: 978-0-9824090-6-0

COVER AND INTERIOR DESIGN: Rita Lascaro
FRONT COVER: Robert Goodnough, *Horses III*, 1960. Collection of Millette and Haag Sherman, Houston, Texas. Courtesy of Langs de Wal Gallery, NY. © Estate of Robert Goodnough.
BACK COVER: Photograph of Robert Goodnough, c. 1950. Courtesy of the Estate of Robert Goodnough.

Contents

Foreword

Robert Goodnough in the 1950s

In my survey of the New York School in the 1950s, I featured Robert Goodnough as one of the dozen or so of its leading younger artists.[1] Goodnough's painting was clearly rooted in his own personal vision. At the same time, it was related to the liveliest vanguard art, or as he put it, "what painting has become."[2]

Goodnough's vision was shaped by his familiarity with the avant-garde art of the late 1940s and 1950s, knowledge that he acquired by way of his friendship with leading artists. In 1949, Goodnough was a graduate student in the studio program at New York University, located in the School of Education along with nursing and health professions.[3] The university evidently differentiated between curriculums based on academic subjects, such as art history, and those that focused on education and hands-on practice. Besides, the art historians in the School of Art and Science did not want to cohabit with artists. But the coupling of artmaking with nursing and the like did not lessen the reputation of NYU's studio program as one of the liveliest in New York. Accountable for

---

1. Goodnough was included twice in *ARTnews*'s annual selection of "Ten Best" one-person shows of the year, that is, in 1958 and 1959. B.H. Friedman's *School of New York: Some Younger Artists* was published in 1959. It featured eleven artists whose work exemplified the taste of the audience for advanced art at the time. In addition to Goodnough, they were Helen Frankenthaler, Grace Hartigan, Jasper Johns, Alfred Leslie, Joan Mitchell, Ray Parker, Robert Rauschenberg, Larry Rivers, Jon Schueler and Richard Stankiewicz.
2. "Is Today's Artist With or Against the Past," *ARTnews*, (Summer 1958): 42.
3. Goodnough studied with Hans Hofmann in 1947.

the course's stature were professors Tony Smith, Hale Woodruff and William Baziotes. They attracted remarkable students, among them Goodnough, Alfred Leslie, Larry Rivers and George Segal, all World War II veterans subsidized by the GI Bill.

In order to provide additional space for their students, Smith, Woodruff and educator Robert Iglehart rented a loft at 35 East 8th Street, a five-minute walk from the university, and named it Studio 35. The space had been occupied previously by The Subjects of the Artist School, whose faculty consisted of Robert Motherwell, William Baziotes, Mark Rothko, David Hare and Barnett Newman. To broaden the course of study, other artists were invited to speak on Friday evenings. The sessions were open to the public and were attended by most everyone interested in avant-garde art, some 150 persons an evening.

Smith, Woodruff and Igelhart decided to continue the public lectures at Studio 35. The task of inviting artists and other organizational chores, such as renting chairs from a nearby funeral parlor, were assumed by Smith, who enlisted Goodnough's help. Indeed, Smith became the young artist's primary mentor and introduced him to friends who were leading Abstract Expressionists, notably Rothko, Newman, Jackson Pollock, and Robert Motherwell. In preparation for his master's thesis, Goodnough interviewed these painters, among others. He also wrote a major article on Pollock for *ARTnews* in 1951.

In 1949, Goodnough was admitted into membership of The Club, a meeting place for the New York School. There he met another group of avant-garde artists, among them Willem de Kooning and Franz Kline, and attended the frequent panels and lectures. Particularly intrigued by Kline, he wrote an article on his work for *ARTnews* in 1952.

In 1950, at the suggestion of Goodnough, and organized by him, Studio 35 convened a three-day closed conference of twenty-five avant-garde artists. Among those included were Motherwell, who was the moderator on the first and third day, Baziotes, Louise Bourgeois, de Kooning, Hans Hofmann, Norman Lewis, Newman, Ad Reinhardt and David Smith, as well as Alfred Barr, the director of the Museum of Modern Art, who chaired the second day. Goodnough shaped and edited the transcript of these sessions, which was published in 1951 in *Modern Artists in America,* whose editorial associates were Motherwell and Reinhardt. The discourse at this conference summed up the thinking of its participants in the late 1940s, notably what they shared as artists. The Studio 35 roundtable was the most important early gathering of the avant-garde, and Goodnough's report turned out to be of exceptional art historical significance.

What did all of these activities contribute to Goodnough the painter? They gave rise to a lively avant-garde ferment in which he was introduced to the latest and most vital art and ideas, and all the fresh options in contemporary art. It was this exposure to avant-garde possibilities that influenced his own work.

In his article on Pollock, Goodnough dealt with the idea that avant-garde painting embodied "an experience of paint and canvas directly, without interference from the suggested forms and colors of existing objects."[4] This idea was very much in the air. For example, Motherwell wrote in 1951, "The process of painting then is conceived of as an adventure, without preconceived ideas. [It] is only by giving oneself up completely to the painting medium that one finds oneself and one's own style."[5] Goodnough's own painting was based on such free improvisation. However, he would add, "I also like to work . . . with discipline."[6]

Abstract Expressionist painters in the 1950s tended to rely more than they had in the previous decade on references to landscape

4. Robert Goodnough, "Pollock paints a picture," *ARTnews* (May 1951): 60.
5. Robert Motherwell, catalog for the exhibition, *The School of New York,* (Beverly Hills, CA: Perls Gallery, 1951): n.p.
6. Robert Goodnough, quoted in Martin H. Bush and Kenworth Moffett, *Goodnough* (Wichita, Kansas: University Art Museum, Wichita State University, 1973): 93.

and the figure. They also drew on earlier art, as Goodnough put it, "the continuity between the past and the present."[7] In keeping with these developments, his abstract images often began with the human figure, as in *Pink Reclining Nude* (1959) and *Standing Figure* (1960). As he said, "I have to paint something, start with some theme, some object to 'transpose.'"[8] Goodnough's images also allude to art historical subjects, such as *Pegasus* (1952) and *Laocoön* (1958). Moreover, in style, his works often look back to Cubist structure as a stabilizer for free-wheeling brushwork, as in *Standing Figure* and *The Struggle* (both of 1957).

Goodnough recalled that in the late 1940s, the Abstract Expressionists he had come to know were developing a sense of independence from the School of Paris. There was a concomitant feeling that they constituted a New York School. Although Goodnough believed that the artists' imagery was not nationalistic, there is a suggestion in his writing on Pollock's painting that it is peculiarly American. As he wrote, Pollock carried "into his painting a sense of freedom experienced before endless mountains and plains, and perhaps this is not surprising in an artist born in Cody, Wyoming . . . and raised in Arizona and northern California."[9]

Tony Smith was more explicit. He said, "We thought about American-ness. . . . We judged art not on the basis of tradition but of our experience. The Europeans considered us barbarians. We said to hell with them. We were going to be what we were, and if it was American, OK."[10] In his own work, Goodnough referred to the history of the United States in *The Frontiersman* (1957) and *Calamity Jane* (1958), among other canvases. In 1958, he wrote, "There is a feeling in the best work of American painters of the 'wild' which has been the heritage of this country. The

7. "Is Today's Artist With or Against the Past," ibid.
8. Ibid.
9. Goodnough, "Pollock paints a picture," 38.
10. Conversation with the author.

covered wagons, the Indians, the rolling prairies, the immense forests and mountains are part of one's memory. Thoreau's belief that dullness and tameness are the same, that is the 'wild' that attracts us in literature, seems also to apply to painting."[11] So it does in Goodnough's work.

Irving Sandler

11. Robert Goodnough, "Statement," *It is* 1 (Spring 1958): 46.

Introduction

In 1950, five years before William Seitz (1914–74) completed his doctoral dissertation "Abstract Expressionist Painting in America" for Princeton University, Robert Goodnough (1917–2010) wrote a similar study, "Subject Matter of the Artist: An Analysis of Contemporary Subject Matter in Painting as Derived from Interviews with those Artists Referred to as the Intrasubjectivists," in partial fulfillment of the requirements for his master's degree in art at New York University. Neither of these pioneering research efforts was published until after the author's death—Seitz's paper appeared as a much-heralded book in 1983, while Goodnough's remained unpublished, and virtually unknown, until now.[1]

Like Seitz, Goodnough was both a scholar and a practicing artist. This allowed the two of them to recognize and analyze the concepts underlying what was then-defined as Abstract Expressionism and/or the New York School. It also enabled them to identify sympathetically with the artists who were at the forefront of those developments. They interviewed several representatives of the movement, three of whom—Willem de Kooning (1904–97), Mark Rothko (1903–70), and Robert Motherwell (1915–91)—spoke to both men.

1. In her notes for the Afterword of *The Turning Point: The Abstract Expressionists and the Transformation of American Art* (New York: Simon & Schuster, 1992), in which Seitz's dissertation is referenced, April Kingsley mentions Goodnough's research paper, but says: "This potentially invaluable document has since, unhappily, been lost." (405)

When Seitz's dissertation was finally published by Harvard University Press, Motherwell contributed a Foreword in which he praised the author's "stunning effort to clarify the actual nature of Abstract Expressionism, a thorough but broad critical analysis of not only what we artists were saying, but more importantly, were painting, the central issue."[2] In Motherwell's retrospective view, Seitz's combination of scholarly rigor and creative practice made his study "a classic—not only in the literature of Abstract Expressionism, but also sui generis in the scholarship of Modernism." (xii) Thus was Goodnough written out of the record by a principal theorist of the movement, who moreover had participated in both research projects.

Motherwell's failure to acknowledge Goodnough's prior contribution—narrower in scope, but no less perceptive—to the study of Abstract Expressionism is all the more baffling in that the two men were far from passing acquaintances. They had worked closely together on Motherwell's *Modern Artists in America* for which Goodnough had organized, transcribed, and edited *Artists' Sessions at Studio 35* (1950). The participants of this artist's forum included five of the seven artists he had interviewed for his paper the previous fall: William Baziotes (1912–63), Adolph Gottlieb (1903–74), Barnett Newman (1905–70), de Kooning, and Motherwell himself. Several of their Studio 35 statements echo the attitudes they expressed in their conversations with Goodnough, who wrote that they "seemed unusually willing to be as honest in the matter as possible and talked earnestly of the problems which were of evident concern to them."

The absence of apparent subject matter in the traditional sense was a primary issue for painters whose imagery lacked representational references, and a problem for those struggling to understand modern art. To many people, non-objective

2. William C. Seitz, *Abstract Expressionist Painting in America*. Cambridge: Harvard University Press, 1983.

painting, whether geometric or gestural, seemed devoid of content. As early as 1943, Gottlieb, Newman, and Rothko wrote a letter to the *New York Times* countering the notion that their art was pure formalism. "There is no such thing as a good painting about nothing," they maintained. "We assert that the subject is crucial."[3] After World War II, as New York gained traction as a center of artistic innovation, Motherwell, Baziotes, Rothko, and the sculptor David Hare (1917–92) founded The Subjects of the Artist School with the purpose of exposing students to "the different subjects of all four artists—to what modern artists paint about, as well as how they paint."[4] Although the experimental school was short-lived (October 1948–May 1949), it reflected a more extensive effort to redefine art's form and function in contemporary culture. It was this search for relevant subject matter, deeply personal and spontaneously generated, that inspired Goodnough's project, which yielded illuminating insights from the artists he interviewed.

As the director and editor of Wittenborn's series Documents of Modern Art, Motherwell was responsible for choosing material for publication. Whether or not he considered including any of Goodnough's research in *Modern Artists in America*—which he coedited with Bernard Karpel (1912–86), the Museum of Modern Art's art librarian, and the painter Ad Reinhardt (1913–67)—the fact that some of the content is similar to what was discussed at the roundtable would likely have disqualified it as redundant. Moreover, the paper itself is organized and presented as an academic study. So "Subject Matter of the Artist" was filed away, although one of Goodnough's conversations became the basis of his May 1951 *ARTnews* article, "Pollock paints a picture." As part

---

3. "Letter to the Editor," *New York Times*, June 13, 1943, national edition.

4. The school's prospectus is reprinted in Kingsley (106). Discussing the school's approach, she quotes one of the students, Yvonne Thomas: "The subject was very real," she recalled, "but no [specific] object was accepted as the basis for the picture. Only subjective feeling." (107)

of the magazine's series about artists' working processes, it is now considered a classic of insightful, sympathetic observation.

The architect and sculptor Tony Smith, one of Goodnough's NYU instructors and a close friend of Pollock's, introduced him to Pollock. "One day," he later wrote, "Smith and Hale Woodruff, who also taught art at NYU, drove out to Springs [on eastern Long Island], with me in the back seat, to visit Pollock," who was then on the wagon. No doubt owing to his sobriety, Pollock "proved to be a very fine, goodhearted, gentle person who didn't talk much but said a lot even by not talking."[5] They then saw each other a few times in New York City, where they had conversations Goodnough subsequently used in his research paper. Evidently, on those occasions, Pollock spoke enough to give Goodnough something with which to work.

The following year, when *ARTnews* editor Thomas B. Hess asked Goodnough, who had been writing reviews for the magazine, "How would you like to do 'Pollock paints a picture'?" he already had the necessary raw material. "Flabbergasted, I thought it over for one tenth of a second—and said yes," he recalled.[6] Interestingly, the painting Goodnough discussed in print—photographed by Hans Namuth and identified as *Number 4, 1950,* now known as *Autumn Rhythm: Number 30, 1950*—is not the one that confronted him in June when he visited Pollock's studio on assignment. The large painting he saw lying on the studio floor, now titled *Number 32, 1950,* is monochromatic black on unprimed canvas. In spite of its higher number, which was assigned later, it was finished by the time Goodnough and the photographer Rudy Burckhardt arrived, and Pollock declined to do any further work

---

5. Robert Goodnough, "Goodnough Paints a Word Picture: Recollections of Pollock and the New York School," in *Goodnough paints a picture* (ex. cat.), Pollock-Krasner House and Study Center, 2002, n.p. Under the care of a local East Hampton physician, Pollock was able to stop drinking for two years, from late 1948 through late 1950.
6. Ibid.

on it. *Autumn Rhythm* was not begun until July or early August, when Namuth documented Pollock as he painted it. According to his own later account, Goodnough did not return to watch the artist at work on *Autumn Rhythm*, but his article describes the application of other colors in addition to black, evidently based on his prior knowledge of Pollock's typical working method. (He did, however, see the finished canvas in Pollock's solo show at the Betty Parsons Gallery in November–December 1950, which he reviewed for the December issue of *ARTnews*.)

"Pollock paints a picture" deals with both the painting process itself and the motivations behind it, while "Subject Matter of the Artist" focuses on identifying the sources of so-called painting material, i.e., content, which is not derived from observation or other external stimuli. The topic was prompted by an exhibition at the Samuel M. Kootz Gallery in September–October 1949 that included work by 12 artists representing the "intrasubjective" tendency in modern painting, as defined by the contemporary Spanish philosopher José Ortega y Gasset (1883–1955). In the August 1949 issue of *Partisan Review*, Ortega outlined the evolution of painting from Giotto to date, characterizing it as a progression from undifferentiated optical representation through perspectival and spatial illusionism to modern non-objective art, which expresses "subjective states through which and by means of which things appear."[7] "After Cézanne," he wrote, "painting only paints ideas—which, certainly, are also objects, but ideal objects, immanent to the subject or intrasubjective."[8]

This approach, independent of external observation and mimetic intent, lies at the core of what was then being defined as the new American painting, although many artists would replace ideas with even more subjective stimuli such as experiences and

7. José Ortega y Gasset, "On Point of View of the Arts," *Partisan Review* 8 (August 1949): 832. This title appears in the magazine on the article's title page; it is listed as "On Point of View in the Arts" in the Table of Contents.
8. Ibid, 833.

emotions. The artist was liberated from representation, but also unmoored from it. In the Kootz Gallery exhibition brochure, the critic Harold Rosenberg (1906–78) summarized the challenge in existential terms: "The modern painter is not inspired by anything visible, but only by something he hasn't seen yet. . . . In short, he begins with nothingness. That is the only thing he copies. The rest he invents."[9]

Goodnough's paper cites the critic Clement Greenberg (1909–94), who argued in his now-famous essay "The Present Prospects of American Painting and Sculpture," in the October 1947 issue of the British journal *Horizon*, that contemporary artists needed to break free of their dependence on European stylistic precedents and American Scene subject matter: "the influence of artiness on the one hand and of the Whitmanesque blowhards on the other." (28) Perhaps owing to his insistence on striking out in a new, thoroughly native direction, Greenberg mentioned Surrealism only in passing, although he allowed that Cubism was an essential precedent.

As Greenberg saw it, the problem facing American artists was the struggle against the limitations of established norms and values. But his argument that the solution was an art "in which an intense detachment informs all" was not supported by the seven

9. Harold Rosenberg, *The Intrasubjectives*, Samuel M. Kootz Gallery, September 14–October 3, 1949. The 12 artists featured were William Baziotes, Willem de Kooning, Arshile Gorky (who had died the previous year), Adolph Gottlieb, Morris Graves, Hans Hofmann, Robert Motherwell, Jackson Pollock, Ad Reinhardt, Mark Rothko, Mark Tobey, and Bradley Walker Tomlin. Although Goodnough states in his Delimitations section of the paper that the number of interviews was determined by the size of the Kootz Gallery group, he did not interview them all. Gorky of course was deceased, and Graves and Tobey were not in New York at the time. But Hofmann, Reinhardt, and Tomlin were. Instead, Goodnough chose to interview Barnett Newman, who was not in *The Intrasubjectives* exhibition. One may speculate that this was due to Newman's close association with Rothko and Gottlieb, his sympathy with the intrasubjective approach, and his role in the formulation of statements and positions that helped define the New York School.

artists in Goodnough's survey. "Only such an art," Greenberg maintained, "resting on rationality but without permitting itself to be rationalized, can adequately answer contemporary life" as an antidote to the "frustrations that ensue from living at the present moment in the history of western civilization." (27) On the contrary, Goodnough's artists were anything but detached. Admittedly the focus of his study is on art's content rather than its formal or theoretical basis—on what it expressed, not how or why it was made. But the motivations he and the artists discussed have more in common with Surrealist-inspired spontaneity than with the kind of Apollonian rationality that Greenberg promoted.

Motherwell said that his painting "comes from imagination and memory." Gottlieb referred to his use of "free association" to reach his subconscious as a source of subject matter. While Newman felt that "painting should go beyond improvisation," he likened his process to that of an instrument maker who "plays his instrument while he is creating it." Baziotes said he worked toward the moment when "the shapes within the canvas achieve their own meaning as images." Rothko aimed to eliminate anything that "would interfere with complete involvement with the particular experience at hand." This sense of immediacy was seconded by Pollock, who depended on "the physical energy of the painting process itself." Personal self-expression was considered paramount. As de Kooning put it, he painted "to satisfy himself only." In the summary of his research results, Goodnough concluded, "though these artists turn to the same source [the subconscious] for subjects, they stress individuality and believe there is as wide a range of subjects as there are personalities involved."

Helen A. Harrison
Eugene V. and Clare E. Thaw Director
Pollock-Krasner House and Study Center
East Hampton, New York
December 2012

Notes and Acknowledgments

This publication was first proposed more than a decade ago, when the Pollock-Krasner House and Study Center presented an exhibition of Robert Goodnough's work, *Goodnough paints a picture.* The exhibition's guest curator Katie Stratis, associate director of The Studio: An Alternative Space for Contemporary Art in Armonk, New York, was instrumental in obtaining a copy of "Subject Matter of the Artist" from the Special Collections and Visual Resources Division of the Getty Research Institute Library, and Goodnough gladly agreed to its publication. Unfortunately, at the time I was unable to find a willing publisher. One of those to whom a proposal was submitted was George Braziller, Inc., where Julia Klein was then employed. As she later wrote to me, the transcript intrigued her, and she subsequently visited Goodnough and his wife Miko at their home in Thornwood, New York. When she started her own imprint, Soberscove Press, she finally was able to bring the project to fruition. This volume is a companion to her first publication, a reprint of *Artists Sessions at Studio 35* (1950). I am deeply grateful for her enthusiasm, advice, editorial acumen, and commitment to presenting Goodnough's pioneering study to the public.

As presented here, "Subject Matter of the Artist" comprises a transcription of the surviving typescript of Goodnough's research paper. Two pages may be missing; the lacunae are indicated in the text. Three additional pages—summaries of the conversations with Baziotes and Pollock, and a partial draft of

"Pollock paints a picture"—were filed with the typescript but are redundant and have not been included. Misspellings and obvious typographical errors have been corrected, except as noted, but Goodnough's variations on the terms "intrasubjective" and "intrasubjectivists" have not been changed. The typescript includes original underlining that has been retained, as well as several passages of underlining by hand that apparently were not done by Goodnough and have not been reproduced. It is now impossible to say who added them, and when. The paper passed through other hands before it was deposited at the Getty. It is published with the gracious permission of Goodnough's widow, Miko Murasaki Goodnough, and their daughter Kathy, whose cooperation is gratefully acknowledged. I also sincerely appreciate the generosity of Milton Esterow, editor and publisher of *ARTnews,* for permission to reprint Goodnough's article, "Pollock paints a picture," from the magazine's May 1951 issue, and of Natalie Edgar for permission to reprint Goodnough's statement from *It is*. I am also thankful to Kristi McGuire for her sensitive editorial contributions.

In September 1965, Goodnough contributed a "postscript" to an *Artforum* special issue on the New York School. I would like to thank *Artforum*'s assistant editor Annie Ochmanek for permission to reprint it. Apart from "Pollock paints a picture," which draws upon but does not reference "Subject Matter of the Artist," it is the only previously published evidence of his NYU research project. It is included here as a preface that summarizes his intentions and reiterates his conclusions. It also highlights the paper's reflection of an "optimistic spirit" among the interviewees, which contradicts the general "pathos and loneliness" expressed in the Studio 35 sessions, and differs from Clement Greenberg's pessimistic outlook for the future of American artists. Also reprinted is Goodnough's statement about his own work from the Spring 1958 issue of *It is,* the de facto house organ of the New York School, expressing his continuing endorsement of the intrasubjective attitude, inflected with another element that he saw as typically American: wildness. The opposite tendency toward refinement, or "finish," as a characteristically French quality, was discussed at Studio 35, and was often applied pejoratively to postwar gestural abstraction in Europe. In his statement, Goodnough endorsed the purportedly untamed nature of American "action painting" that distinguished it from its more polished European counterparts, l'art informel and tachisme. Like jazz, it represented a primitivistic stereotype that both appalled and fascinated Old World cultural arbiters. In the spirit of Les Fauves, the iconoclastic "wild beasts" of the early-twentieth-century European avant garde, American painters embraced that image.

HAH

"Postscript: The Forties"

Artforum 4, no. 1 (September 1965): 32.

Having been asked to write about the period during the late forties and fifties and since memory is not always accurate in details and the proper order of things as they happened, I am referring somewhat to a paper I wrote in 1950 for a course at New York University—called "Subject Matter of the Artist." The term "subject matter" can be misleading when referring to abstract painting but it was then used to convey the meaning that the artist may have a subject even if it does not refer directly to recognizable objects or incidents; that his attempts to deal with more subjective feelings and ideas constitute subjects. I had been in New York only a short time but found the artists to be enthusiastic and quite involved in finding their own direction, with a kind of new independence from the Paris[ian] influence that was giving impetus to their work. To quote from the paper mentioned,

> American artists have been characterized either by noticeable foreign influence or by reaction to this influence. When there was no access to what was being done abroad (during the last war) and no desire to emulate the work of previous American artists, some artists felt there was nothing left to do but turn to themselves to seek development. They were left on their own. They did not believe art was nationalistic,

> but rather universal; it should deal only with a language that might have meaning anywhere. Yet they felt that art did depend on subject matter and that the source of the subject was important, and, since landscape and figure painting had been dealt with to the extent of no longer being interesting or meaningful for contemporary expression, they began to try to find new subjects which might be available through the subconscious mind.

This was my interpretation of the attitude of mind of those artists I knew who were in some way then connected with "Studio 35." I interviewed William Baziotes, Mark Rothko, Willem de Kooning, Jackson Pollock, Adolph Gottlieb, Robert Motherwell, and Barnett Newman. They all seemed to feel optimistic and enthusiastic and there was a good feeling that seemed to pervade the art world. While each artist acted as an individual and had more or less his own direction, there was a strong group spirit that apparently arose from the European scene and the idea that a New York school was emerging. I mention this optimistic spirit because that is what I most clearly recall from those years. After the impetus of that time the group began gradually to separate and go their separate ways and while many things have been happening since, I am not aware of the same strong sense of direction (though this may be because I now work more on my own).

Subject Matter of the Artist:

An analysis of contemporary subject matter in painting as derived from interviews with those artists referred to as the intrasubjectivists

Submitted to meet requirements for the course in Research in Design directed by Doctor George Ross at the School of Education of New York University, 1950

Preface

As a painter and as one interested in education in relation to painting and drawing, the writer has become personally interested in the problem of subject matter in art. Since much of the painting done today is characterized by the absence of recognizable subjects, controversy has arisen as to what the artist is concerned with as subject matter and his attitude toward what he is doing when he finds it necessary to eliminate objects which may be identified as derived from things already in existence. The writer's interest has been further strengthened by contact with many competent artists who work in this way, and he feels that education in art would be aided by clarification of the issues involved. These issues, it is felt, may best come to light if the personal attitudes of some of these artists are made clear.

The assistance of Mr. Robert Iglehart, Mr. Anthony Smith, and Dr. George Ross, all teachers at New York University, is deeply appreciated. The artists whose interviews appear in this paper seemed unusually willing to be as honest in the matter as possible and talked earnestly of the problems which were of evident concern to them.

Part I

Introduction

THE PROBLEM

The purpose in this investigation is to deal with new attitudes toward subject matter as evidenced in the work of certain contemporary artists who have eliminated recognizable objects as a means for expression in painting.

APPROACH TO THE PROBLEM

Recently, an exhibition held in New York brought together examples of work by a group of artists termed the "intrasubjectivists." There was a noticeable lack of recognizable objects in the paintings and little attempt to deal with space in three dimensions. Most of the artists in the group are represented in the Museum of Modern Art and numerous museums throughout the country and abroad and are therefore accepted for the purposes of the paper as outstanding in the art field. Since there is controversy in regards to this tendency in painting, research directed toward the source of ideas involved in the work, it is felt, will help to make clear the intention of the artists. This research will deal with the attitudes of these artists toward their own work and their relation to tradition as they express it.

INTERVIEWS

In the attempt to come as close to the problem as possible, it was felt that personal interviews with the artists would most nearly give a valid picture of what is being attempted and of the issues these men consider to be important.

DELIMITATIONS

The interviews were held with artists in New York City during the latter part of the year nineteen hundred forty-nine. Only artists concerned with the intrasubjective, and who were available for questioning, were included. The nature of the problem is such that personal contacts with the men concerned were considered necessary. The number of interviews was determined by the size of the group of intrasubjectivists who exhibited at the Kootz Gallery, 600 Madison Avenue, New York City, from September fourteenth through October third, nineteen hundred forty-nine.

HYPOTHESIS

It may be expected that there will be agreement among the artists as to the source of ideas they use in painting, since their paintings are generally characterized by the elimination of recognizable objects. While there is similarity in approach to painting within this group, the work of the individual artists differs widely, and they may also stress the importance of variation in painting in relation to personalities.

DEFINITION OF TERMS

The word art is accepted as meaning those creations of men which arouse emotions pertaining to the beautiful, especially as distinguished from the useful.

Because of its general acceptance in identifying pictures containing forms not recognizable or nearly indiscernable, the term abstract is here used in that sense. In its proper sense, abstract art is considered to refer to works in which the forms are abstracted, or selected, from objects already in existence, and the term should not refer to works not having reference to existing objects.

Automatic applies to actions performed without conscious or willed direction, as related to painting. An automatic image is an image or form which develops without conscious direction.

Consciousness is used as meaning critical awareness.

Objects are referred to as things existing outside the sense organs but to which the sense organs may react.

Non-objective is the term applied to works containing no object. However it usually does not take subject matter into account.

The term subject matter is considered to mean that in a painting which causes emotional reaction in the observer. Forms referring to existing objects and forms derived from the subconscious are included in the term. Content is used as synonymous with the subject matter.

Subconscious is used as having to do with mental operations which are not present in the consciousness.

Subjective is accepted as that belonging to reality as perceived or known, as opposed to reality independent of mind, and resulting from conditions within the brain and sense organs.

The word intrasubjective is accepted as meaning that which is within the subjective mind, where perception and awareness takes place, and as a realm of experience common to all human beings. It is believed that there is here a meeting ground of common understanding. Where the term is used as a name for the artists represented in this paper, it is capitalized. The content of consciousness is considered to be synonymous with intrasubjective.

A symbol is that which suggests something else by reason of relationship. A form is any discernable shape which may, or may not, have associative meaning or be recognizable.

The term painting material is used in certain cases as meaning ideas to deal with in painting. This will appear evident in the context.

HISTORY

In order to clarify the problem dealt with in this paper, a brief history of the object as used in painting, based on the complete article by José Ortega y Gasset, is here presented.[1]

1. José Ortega y Gasset, "On Point of View of the Arts," *Partisian Review* 8 (August 1949).

Ortega shows the history of painting to be a gradual development from the visual expression of object as having bulk, through attention to the surface of objects and an awareness of the importance of the space between the eye and the object, and finally the elimination of the object and a reversal of the pattern of experience into the eye itself, or, into the mind of the artist. He explains that Giotto painted solid and separate bodies, coinciding with [the] philosophic[al] thinking of the time, for ultimate reality was then believed to be best understood in terms of individual substances. Each object was felt to have an existence of its own and to be perfect in itself according to its inner energy. At about the year sixteen hundred, the painting of hollow space began. Simultaneously, Descartes spoke of a single substance and metaphysical empty space became the means of philosophical explanation of reality. Here objects are not painted as seen, but rather the experience of seeing is painted. The background is brought forward and an approximation of the original plane of the canvas is achieved. Art begins to withdraw from the natural world and to be concerned with the sensations and activity of the subject, the artist. Sensations become subjective states by means of which things appear.

Subjectivism becomes more radical and at the end of the nineteenth century, while the positivists in philosophy reduce philosophy to pure sensations, the impressionists also attempt to deal with sensations in as pure a way as possible.

The "content of consciousness" or the intrasubjective, becomes the problem of contemporary philosophic and artistic research. After Cézanne, painting is concerned only with ideas. Even the volumes of Cézanne, which may at first appear as similar to the masses of Giotto, become not the actual volumes which Giotto tried to render, but non-existent volumes of Cézanne's own creation.

It is in dealing with the "content of consciousness" that the language of contemporary expression seeks to reconstruct the world. This tendency toward inward exploration appears in numerous cases. The artist now often attempts to create paintings which are self-existent, without associations, value or illusion, without relation even to the walls on which they might hang, as free as billboards. Writers are often concerned with subjective processes and with the "stream of consciousness."

RECENT HISTORY

Clement Greenberg gives a picture of the problems confronting the contemporary American artist.[2] His analysis was also upheld by Adolph Gottlieb during the interview for this paper. They explain that during the last war a definite change in painting sprang up in America which has developed to the point of making itself felt in the art world. Little work from Europe was available when this movement started. At the same time, many felt dissatisfaction with paintings of the American scene and paintings dealing with social content. American artists have usually been influenced to a large extent by painting in Europe, especially Paris, and much of the work has been characterized either by noticeable foreign influence or by reaction to this influence. When there was no access to what was being done abroad, and no desire to emulate the work of previous American artists, some artists felt there was nothing left to do but turn to themselves to seek development. They were left on their own. They did not believe art was nationalistic, but rather universal; it should not display the glories of Paris or of this country but should deal only with a language that might have meaning anywhere. Yet they felt that art did depend on subject matter and that the source of the subject was important, and, since landscape and figure painting had been dealt with to the extent of no longer being interesting or meaningful for contemporary expression, they began to try to find [a] new subject which might be available through turning to the subconscious mind.

---

2. Clement Greenberg, "[The Present Prospects of] American Painting and Sculpture," *Horizon*, 93–94 (October 1947): 20–30.

In a comprehensive view of new attitudes of men toward their environment, Paul Valéry notes a fact of outstanding significance, which by its greatness and obviousness has almost gone unnoticed. He states,

> The entire habitable globe has now been explored, seized, and shared among nations. The age of uncharted areas, of unoccupied territories, of places which nobody owns, and therefore the age of free expansion, is at an end. There is not a rock without its flag, there are no mere blanks on the map, no region beyond law and custom, not a tribe whose affairs do not give birth to some dossier and do not depend, through the maleficent powers of the pen, upon various remote humanists in their offices. The age of a finite world is now beginning.[3]

In connection with this he later asked if it is possible to "from now on, act, think, write, and live as if what is to come cannot hope to be expressed in terms of what was, and cannot be made intelligible or be usefully defined by what has been." [4]

3. Paul Valéry, *Reflections on the World Today* (Pantheon 1948): 21–22.
4. Ibid, 139.

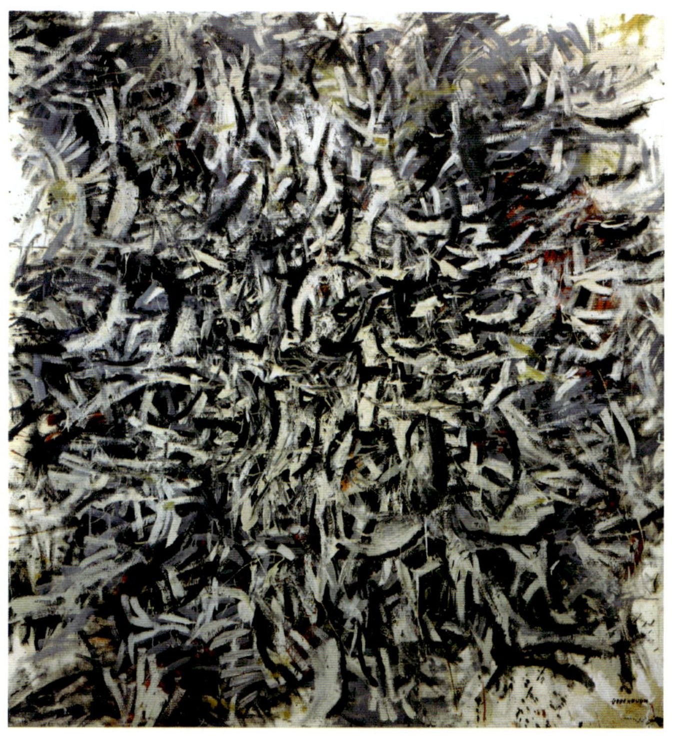

Robert Goodnough, *Abstraction,* 1953. Oil on canvas, 53 x 53 inches. © Estate of Robert Goodnough

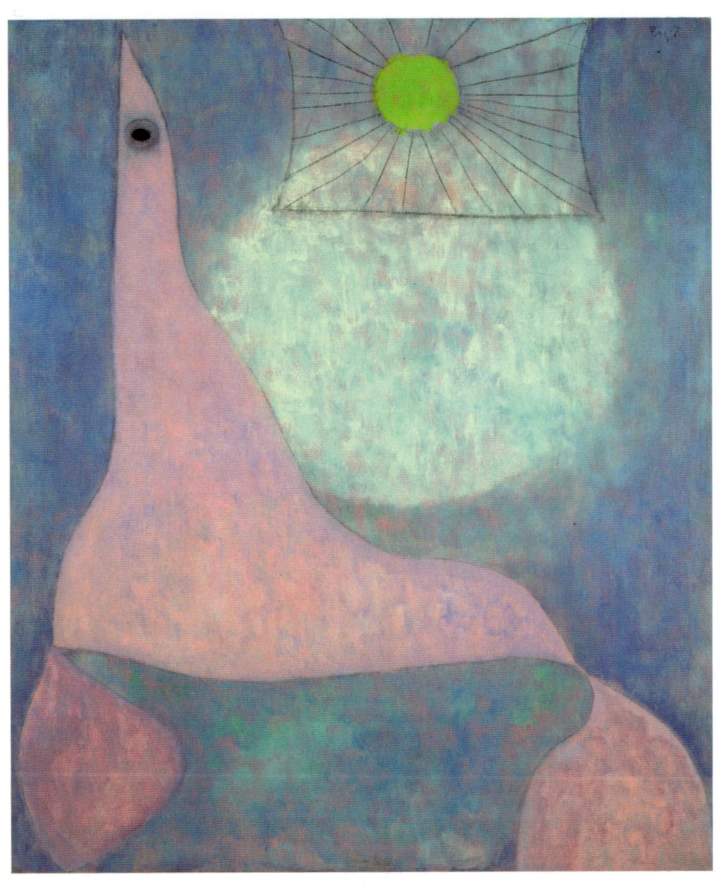

William Baziotes, *Moon Animal*, 1950. Oil on canvas, 43 x 36 1/4 inches. Krannert Art Museum and Kinkead Pavilion, University of Illinois at Urbana-Champaign. Festival of Arts Purchase Fund, 1951-6-1. Digital image courtesy of Krannert Art Museum.

Mark Rothko (American, born Russia, 1903–1970), *Untitled 1949*. Oil on canvas, 81 3/8 x 66 3/8 inches. National Gallery of Art, Washington, D.C. Gift of The Mark Rothko Foundation, Inc. 1986.43.138. Digital Image licensed by the National Gallery of Art. © 1998 Kate Rothko Prizel & Christopher Rothko/Artists Rights Society (ARS), New York.

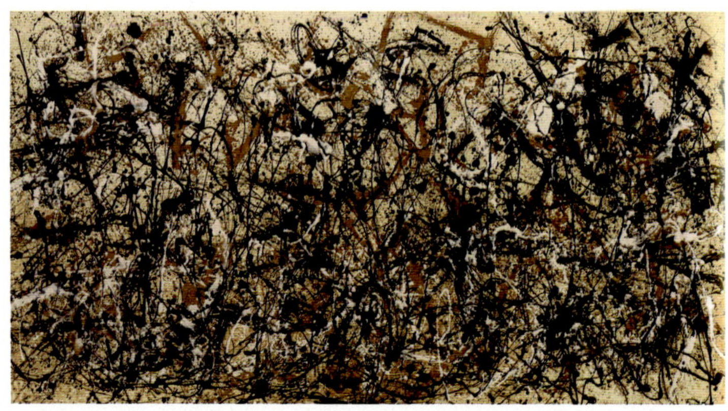

Jackson Pollock, *Autumn Rhythm: Number 30, 1950*. Enamel on canvas, 8 feet 9 inches x 17 feet 3 inches. Metropolitan Museum of Art, New York. George A. Hearn Fund, 1957.

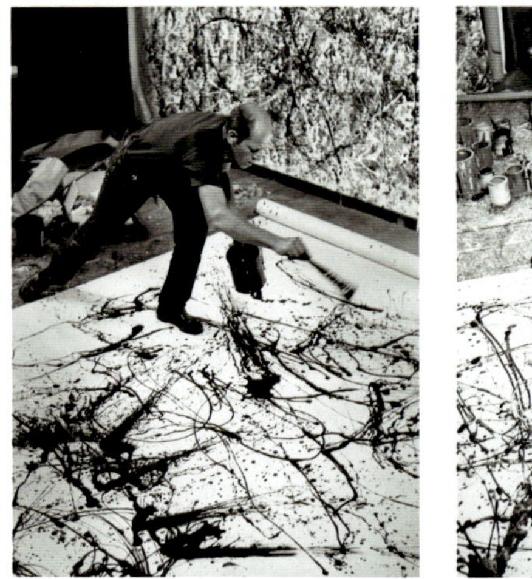

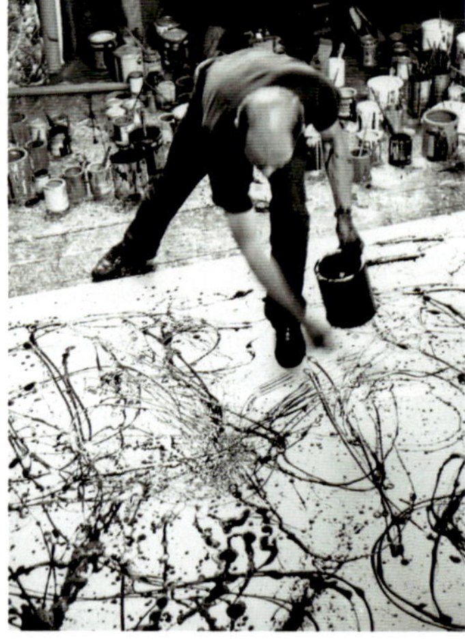

Hans Namuth, Jackson Pollock painting *Autumn Rhythm*, 1950.

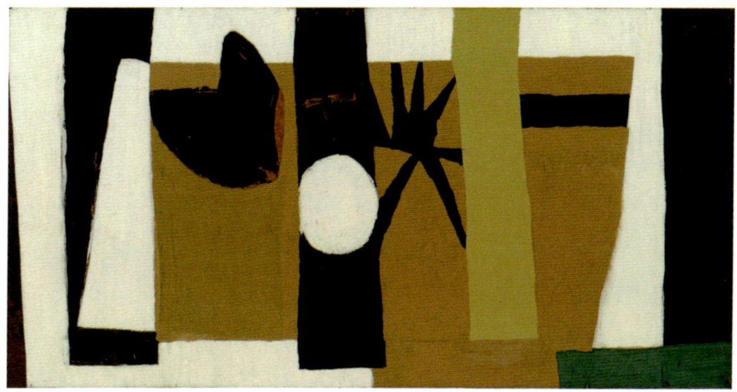

Robert Motherwell, *The Voyage,* 1949. Oil, tempera, and charcoal on paper mounted on masonite, 48 x 94 inches. Museum of Modern Art, New York. Gift of Mrs. John D. Rockefeller III. Digital Image © Museum of Modern Art, licensed by SCALA/Art Resource. Art © Dedalus Foundation, Inc./Licensed by VAGA, New York, NY.

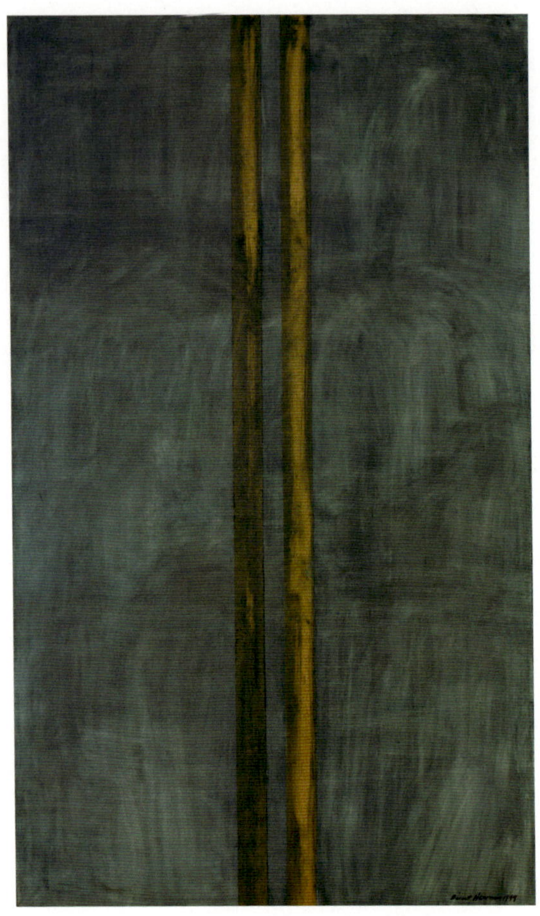

Barnett Newman, *Concord*, 1949. Oil and masking tape on canvas, 89¾ x 53⅝ inches. Metropolitan Museum of Art, New York. George A. Hearn Fund, 1968 (68.178). Digital Image © Metropolitan Museum of Art, licensed by SCALA/Art Resource. © 2013 The Barnett Newman Foundation, New York/Artists Rights Society (ARS), New York.

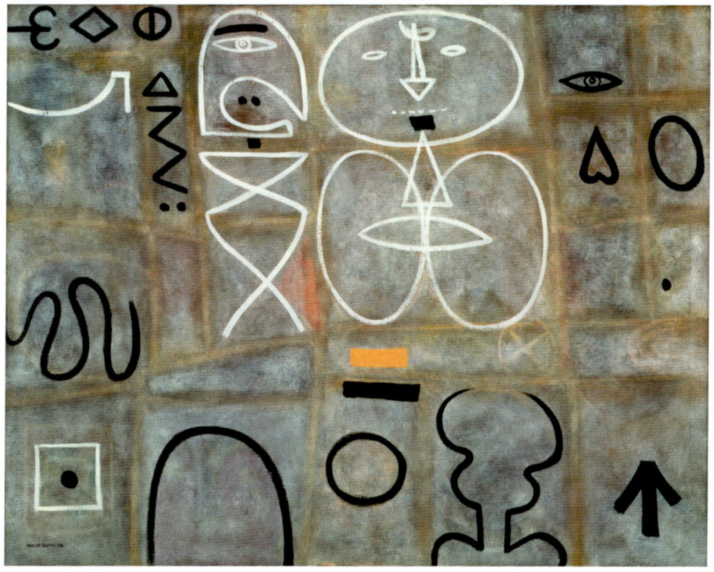

Adolph Gottlieb, *Man Looking at Woman*, 1949. Oil on canvas, 42 x 54 inches. Museum of Modern Art, New York. Gift of the artist. Digital Image © Museum of Modern Art, licensed by SCALA/Art Resource. Art © Adolph and Esther Gottlieb Foundation/ Licensed by VAGA, New York, NY.

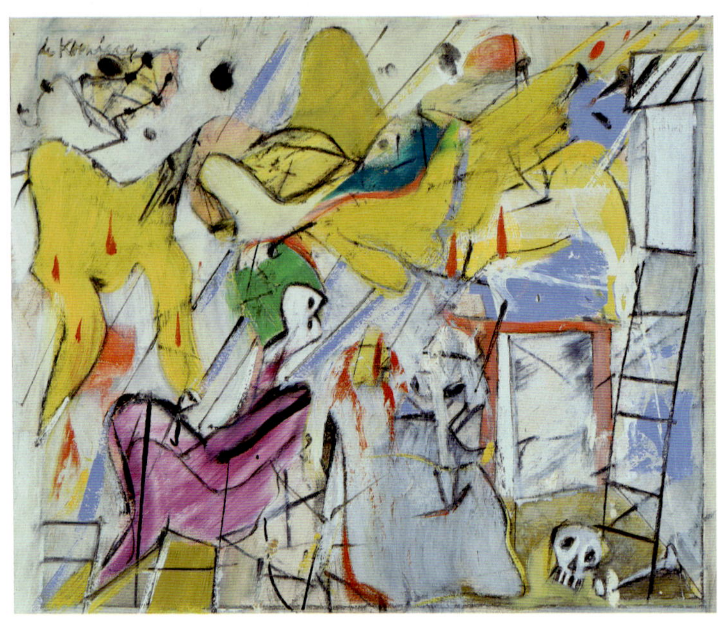

Willem de Kooning, *Abstraction*, 1949–50. Oil and oleoresin on cardboard, $16\frac{1}{8}$ x $19\frac{1}{4}$ inches. Museo Thyssen-Bornemisza, Madrid. Digital Image © Museo Thyssen-Bornemisza, Madrid, licensed by SCALA/Art Resource. © 2013 The Willem de Kooning Foundation/Artists Rights Society (ARS), New York.

Part II

Interviews with the Artists

The statements in the interviews presented in this section are given as the artists made them and all thoughts expressed are those of the artists themselves. The analysis made by the writer follows each interview.

PROCEDURE

The artists represented in this paper were interviewed in the latter part of nineteen forty-nine in New York City. For reference material only, writings were chosen which dealt directly with the intrasubjectivists, or lead to them historically.

The writer feels that by limiting the problem in this way, and by concentrating on the personal points of view of the artists, a more revealing picture results.

After the interviews were written up, each one was analyzed to show the important points in the content, and a final summary was made to cover the information derived.

During the interviews, informal questions were directed toward causing the artists to reveal their own attitudes about their work and the work of the men of the group. The artists were questioned as to why existing objects were not referred to as painting material, and they were asked to clarify their ideas about subject matter in painting and the source of this subject matter.

Photographs of the work of these artists were collected, partially from the magazine called "The Tiger's Eye," to give an idea of how the artists work.[5]

NEED FOR THE STUDY

José Ortega y Gasset has adequately anticipated the need for examination of this problem in an article giving a history of the relation of the object to painting. At the end of this article he asks where material may be found to reconstruct the world. He says,

> The philosopher retracts his attention even more and fixes on what up to now has been called 'the content of consciousness,' that is, the intrasubjective. There may be no corresponding reality to what ideas project and what thoughts think, but this does not make them purely subjective. A world of hallucination would not be real, but neither would it fail to be a world, an objective universe, full of sense and perfection.[6]

He does not make clear what is included in the intrasubjective, but the problem arises as to how this may be dealt with by the artists.

There does not seem to be a clear understanding of what is involved in approaching painting with no reference to existing objects. Art teachers often confuse the issue by a lack of awareness of the significance of this kind of painting, and thereby do not make clear to their students what is important in this way of working.

---

5. Since the typescript does not indicate the titles of these works, each artist is represented here by an example from the period.
6. José Ortega y Gasset, "On Point of View of the Arts," *Partisian Review* 8 (August 1949): 836.

William Baziotes

FROM AN INTERVIEW

William Baziotes seeks, by dealing with poetic emotion, to awaken a response through his paintings which is outside the prosaic or banal experience of daily life. Good paintings always move people in this way. He started by painting landscapes and figures which became more and more abstract until direct contact with objects, as related to his subject matter, ceased altogether. Since he wanted more imaginative effects not hampered by anatomical meaning, he was led to distortion first and then to the elimination of objects. In nineteen-forty Baziotes faced a difficult period in his work. He was unable to complete a canvas, though he worked on one for a year. He finally took hold of himself, made hundreds of drawings and disciplined himself by using small canvases. Out of this came a decided change in his work and the beginning of his present direction, and since then his painting has been a continuous fight, with changes happening gradually.

Baziotes now works without sketches or previous preparation. He sets down a series of impressions on his canvas and works with them until they being to crystallize and the canvas "begins to speak" to him. On a particular day he may set up a number of canvases that he is working on and see which he reacts to. This gives him a clue about what what he is like that day and the other canvases are put aside until he feels closer to them. In this way his paintings gradually build up until the time when they take on their own life and the shapes within the canvas achieve their own meanings as images.

While he is related to the group of non-representational painters, Baziotes points out that this group should not be called a school of painting since a school would consist of a leading painter and those who follow his influences. There is a wide diversity within this group and, while the artists learn from each other, each believes in his own rights as an individual.

"Reference to existing objects is not particularly helpful in contemporary painting," Baziotes says. Art passes through periods in which certain aspects predominate; at one time realism may be stressed, at another time religious painting will dominate. Today the painters tend to deal with subjective feelings. Thus art goes through continual changes and becomes manifest by different means at different times. There is nothing mystical in contemporary painting, to Baziotes. The present tendency of many artists to eliminate objects is in line with this tradition. By viewing painting from Cézanne to the present, we find a gradual development toward abstraction or toward what might more nearly be termed a broader view of content. There is then no break with tradition. Baziotes says, "but only the logical development of painting, which is in keeping with the times."

ANALYSIS

The elimination of objects is in line with tradition, but rather than eliminating content, gives way to a more comprehensive conception of what content is.

The method of setting down a series of impressions on a canvas, without previous preparation, and then waiting for the canvas to "speak" to him, suggests an attempt on Baziotes's part to find his subject matter through giving direct attention to the subconscious, and allowing it to determine his subject.

Mark Rothko

FROM AN INTERVIEW

Mark Rothko began painting when he was twenty-four. Until that time he had not been interested in painting or in museums, although he had a sculptor friend whose problems he listened to but could not understand. As an interest in painting began to appear, he visited the museums but found that the paintings did not move him as he was moved by music. Yet he found that the feeling persisted that something akin to the emotional intensity of great music might be achieved in painting. He began to paint seriously, even studying with Max Weber for two months, but found that the figures he was using in his canvases were becoming more and more distorted. He finally decided that the conclusion of this distortion was to eliminate figures from his canvases altogether. There followed a period of interest in symbols and myths, which he dealt with as forms on the canvases tying them in with dark lines.

Rothko chose Mozart as an example of clarity of idea which continues through his compositions, clear in that there is not feeling of nostalgia or of reference to previous experience. Clarity then began to depend, to Rothko, on the elimination of anything in his work which might deal with association or remind one of previous attachments since any outside experience would interfere with complete involvement with the particular experience at hand.

Rothko stresses the fact that he desires to do paintings which achieve complete clarity of idea, in which there can be no doubt as to intention. In the attempt to achieve this impact he strives to eliminate all negative factors, anything which might interfere with the newness of experience he feels to be important in creative activity. The figure, though distorted, still was tied to the past and had to be eliminated. Symbols could only be meaningful by association and interfered with clearness. And since space is a part of experience, his lines, which appeared to be floating in space, must go. Finally any reference to an illusion of space had to be eliminated.

With the elimination of those elements which hinder the attainment of clarity, Rothko enters a field of experience having little to do with the past or the nostalgic. Space as such is not considered, and even then, becomes an attempt to discover the manner in which this may be most adequately achieved. In that, he seeks a more comprehensive content. Rothko does not consider himself an abstract painter.

To work as Rothko does means to leave behind all familiar ground, to face the wilderness of ideas much as the early settler was faced with the wild of a new continent. Sometimes there is a longing for the homeland, a foothold, a place of security, and yet such security can only inhibit a transcendental experience.

ANALYSIS

Rothko says that he is interested in content, and, since his paintings contain no recognizable objects, but rather depend on large areas of color, it is apparent that he does not consider the content of a painting to be dependent on objects.

The desire to eliminate nostalgic reference or any distraction, which might come through association by causing the observer to remember previous experiences, implies that emotional impact depends on lack of association.

Clarity of idea and emotional impact are dependent on content but not on association. Thus the color relationships become incidental to the nature of the picture image with which he is occupied. The image is presented in terms of the total canvas, and Rothko desires to eliminate any distracting awareness of paint by applying his colors without texture. The impact of the work must be immediate, must "hit one in the belly," and the painting be seen as a totality and a new experience. Mondrian wrote that he was interested in showing that which is the essence of nature, and the vertical and horizontal lines of his painting deal with those relationships as he saw them in nature. The image Rothko is after cannot be realized by this form of structural relationships, but structure itself only has meaning as that which makes a particular picture possible. Structure is not sought but is there, as it is in any work which is capable of moving us. A cubistic picture refers to the structure of existing objects and therefore, to Rothko, deals with association.

Since a painting cannot have emotional impact without content, Rothko feels that his content widens to cover a total experience. He wishes the observer not to find a portion of himself involved but to be totally involved to the exclusion of everything else. His painting exists. A painting may be as real if composed of forms having no references. To avoid the use of objects does not mean to avoid reality but to view reality in a different way.

Jackson Pollock

FROM CONVERSATIONS WITH THE ARTIST

Jackson Pollock paints in a barn in the village of Springs, Long Island. He is a native of Wyoming. Though he studied with Thomas Benton for a while, he soon left the Benton influence and went through periods of intense struggle with his canvases. Though he had not read Dante, he is aware that this earlier work sometimes has the feeling of the "Inferno." He called his paintings "Lucifer," "The She-Wolf," and similar[ly] suggestive titles.

Gradually these ideas have changed and recognizable objects have been eliminated and he depends on forces and tensions produced through the use of paint; the physical energy of the painting process itself becoming of great importance.

To "get into the painting," Pollock lays the canvas on the floor, walks around it and pours paint directly from cans [on]to the unstretched and unsized surface of the canvas. When the painting is started, he tacks it to the wall of his studio and goes through a period of "getting acquainted with it." He feels that the creative development of the artist should determine his means of expression and that the artist should be free to choose those materials most suited to him and to use them as he pleases. The painter should throw away his handbook on materials and discover his own way of using paint, or whatever material he feels most at home with.

Pollock feels that it is not necessary for the painter to verbalize much about his work. It is important for the artist to keep working and what he paints is what will tell in the long run, not what he says about what he does.

ANALYSIS

Forces and tensions, and the physical act of applying paint to the canvas seem to direct Pollock to his subject.

Since he sets up his canvas to become acquainted with it, it appears at this time he becomes aware of the subject which will carry the painting to a complete expression capable of awakening intense emotions in the observers.

Robert Motherwell

FROM AN INTERVIEW

The good painter knows painting and its development and is therefore able to see his own work in relation to what has already been done. Painting does not come so much from looking at nature as from looking at other paintings, Motherwell believes. At the same time he sees painting as a transformation of the desire to paint human beings, the desire of painters to produce independent objects often "forcing a change in attitude toward the figure as material for painting."

When young, Motherwell copied the old masters, Rembrandt, Michelangelo, and others, and in this way acquired his understanding of the nature of painting. Since he never spent hours copying models and still life groups in art classes, he feels that the problem of representation, which may hinder many, does not arise with him. It seems queer to him to draw from nature. His painting comes from imagination and memory. As a conceptual painter he uses whatever may help in the realization of his idea, and if this includes the use of forms that may suggest recognizable objects or symbols, he does not hesitate to use them. The question of whether a form is recognizable or not is beside the point. Most abstract painting he considers to be inferior work. If his own work is not going well, Motherwell is able to set it aside and do something else without becoming emotionally upset.

Motherwell finds that he is more interested in the city street than in nature. He feels this has become more real in contemporary life. The hardness and flatness of the sidewalk and the activity of the city are close to the lives of many and there is greater understanding of what is man made than there is of nature. Motherwell says that his painting is essentially like a wall, and that in his most successful works there is the feeling of flatness, which he does not consciously strive for but which he feels to be characteristic of his work.

In this country Motherwell finds no painters who have yet achieved the stature of the older European artists. Yet the painters here who hold promise are young and in search of maturity, liberation, and subtility [*sic*] of thought, and they are not afraid to paint as they feel. Each seeks his own identity and there is the feeling of "full steam ahead." They are independent but know the importance of the art of Europe and the potentialities of America. The good painters are always individualists. A number of painters may find some common outlook or belief and may associate enough to form a group. This may come about in the manner of a military alliance, to face opposition to what the group is struggling to achieve, as happened in impressionism. When the alliance has served its purpose, it disbands. Within the present group of intrasubjective painters there are many ways of expression and a stress on the importance of individuality. When the group no longer exists the artists must still stand as individuals.

These artists seek that which will liberate them, something new and fresh that is meaningful to them. What they understand in common, according to Motherwell, is that painting is relational structure. All reject what is called "carpenter construction," or an attempt at construction in the three-dimensional sense as a carpenter builds, as this gives an illusion of space that is not in the canvas. The structure of the picture is a part of the idea itself and cannot be separated from it. The work of these artists becomes "a lyrical cry, a shriek, at times a form of humor, but there is no concern with outside incidents or events. There is no intention of manufacturing what people want."

Motherwell feels that the group may actually be called a group of fanatics and it is for this reason that they will succeed. Only to the degree that one is fanatical about an idea is he successful with it and only the fanatic accomplishes work of value. There must be total indifference to how far behind the public is and there must be no concessions.

It is pointed out by Motherwell that few of these artists are able to make a living with their work and yet are so absorbed in what they believe that they continue to work regardless of personal difficulties, showing sincerity of purpose which may be admired. Also there is a high degree of intelligence among these artists. They can talk intelligently and write well about what they are doing, and possess a humility of attitude toward the continual process of search and discovery.

ANALYSIS

Imagination and memory play an important part in Motherwell's painting. A form which suggests an existing object may be used or not depending on whether it helps in the realization of an idea. Thus subject matter does not seem to depend on recognizable objects though they may sometimes help in making the subject evident.

Subject matter does not depend on "drawing from nature" but on what may be raised from the imagination and the subconscious.

Painting today depends on painting of the past and an autonomous development of painting is suggested by Motherwell, the subject matter of which is not determined by the presence or absence of recognizable forms.

Barnett Newman

FROM AN INTERVIEW

Newman believes the artist is a person in exile. "I believe in exile," he says, "a self-imposed exile. As I, as artist, am separate from the world, so a picture is separate from the world of things."

The composer makes diagrams for someone to read. The painter is not a "maker of diagrams." The painter, in a sense, has to make an instrument and to play it at the same time. The voice may be an instrument, and Shakespeare, who was also an actor, integrated what he wrote with vocal expression. He knew how his words would sound on the stage and his process of writing was such that words were felt as "acted words" when written. It is likely that he acted out his parts as he was writing them. This same kind of involvement is what the painter experiences. He has to take a brush and "fight it out" and is about the only one left who works with composing and acting at the same time. The act of painting and the bringing into existence of an art object are one and the same process. In music, a diagram is first created, then it is played on an instrument. The painter plays his instrument while he is creating it.

Newman's painting has developed to a simplified means of expression. He often paints canvases in one flat color with a shiny line down the middle of the same color.[7] He does not agree with

7. The first page of the Newman interview is hand-numbered 39, and the following page (beginning "He does not agree. . . .") is hand-numbered 41, so there may be a page missing, or the pages may be incorrectly numbered.

the idea of attempting to make an automatic image, feeling that this often becomes improvisation. Painting should go beyond improvisation.

The subject matter used by Newman does not come from visible objects or particular events. These are eliminated in the attempt to "create and play an instrument."

ANALYSIS

While Newman paints canvases containing no recognizable forms, he does not believe in automatic painting in which the process becomes a matter of improvisation.

The statement that the picture is "separate from the world of things," even as the artist is, again implies that painting is not concerned with things as they exist.

The artist struggling with his canvas is what matters, without the intervention of a third element, or objects to be represented.

Adolph Gottlieb

FROM AN INTERVIEW

Adolph Gottlieb painted from the model for many years but finally found he could work much more effectively from imagination and memory. After a period of imaginative painting, he again went back to the model and was able to bring a much more interesting handling to it, or could paint his memory of the model in a more exciting way. Finally he conceived of the idea of using different subject matter entirely, of using something which in no way came from reference to the model or to nature. This was a deliberate act on his part to satisfy an unconscious need. He decided to use rectangular compartments in his canvases in order to project different images on a single surface. At first he thought he was selecting significant parts of objects [to] evoke images, those having emotional meaning to him, but later he found he was using images not as parts of existing objects but as coming from a subconscious source, and he felt it was inevitable that he should use them.

Gottlieb always felt that he was an artist but was even more confident of this when younger. Now he realizes that this confidence rested in not [*illegible marginal note*] taking chances. He would now like to make something he is not so sure is art in the accepted sense. "When you do not depend on tradition," he says, "you must develop a new kind of assurance which depends on your own capacities." Academic art stems from a lack of this kind of security, according to Gottlieb. He starts with a fairly clear idea for a painting, but in the process of painting something different may be done with the idea though not to the extent of losing what he started with. He works from sketches, developing them on large canvases, but likes to forget the sketch in the process of the painting and "surprise" himself. He goes through periods of difficulty with his work, after which he notices a "jump" ahead, and though disturbing, they lead to the exciting advancement which makes painting worth while. He feels that his work is influenced by Assyrian art.

Painters of the American Scene such as Wood, Curry, and Benton, Gottlieb named as inferior artists reacting against European art in an immature way. He feels that reaction should not be against good art but only against that which is bad. It is not the artist's problem to try to disqualify work which is good, though he may try to escape its influence. The social painters including Gropper, Evergood, Shahn, and Gwathmey were close to the American Scene artists but tried to give the scene an uplift by introducing social ideas, and only produced scenic subject matter with a social slant. Both of these were a rejection of the significant developments in modern art. Marin, Hartley, and Weber were named as men accepting the whole conception of modern painting but never becoming free enough. Weber was eclectic, always giving the feeling [*illegible marginal note*] of trying to maintain a position during his periods of influence.

When nationalistic and regional art began to die out, then each artist's work had to rest on its own merit and this test, Gottlieb feels, was not easily withstood by many of these men. They were all affected by European domination. Either it was felt necessary to try and disqualify European art, or to copy it. The French were chauvinistic and the American artists were "taken in." Then too, there was American prejudice against American art, probably coming from commercial sources. Thus, many factors led to a reactionary art in this country. Only when there was not much European art available, during the last war, was there a definite attempt at a new universal painting depending on the merit of individual artists.

During the time of social painting, a small but active group sprang up called the American Abstract Artists. Their work was influenced by Mondrian and was non-objective in that [it] eliminate[d] association with natural objects. Gottlieb feels that their work became academic and "began to take painting up a dead-end street." Mondrian's value does not lie in lack of association, but in his purity. It is usually a mistake, Gottlieb says, to try to follow the non-objective trend. Actually, Gottlieb believes that association must be a part of all painting, that this should be recognized, and that artists should become aware that it is the kind of association that is important. There may be association in terms of inward experience as well as that which is outside of human beings. The early [*illegible marginal note*] Pollock paintings and those of Rothko, as well as Gottlieb's own work, rejected the non-objective point of view and Gottlieb finds it curious that some artists are again taking up the non-objective.

Gottlieb uses what he calls "free association," putting down circles and allowing them to suggest other things, perhaps squares or triangles. This offers a way of reaching his subconscious and becomes his subject matter. The subject matter which comes from this process he considers to be very important. The academic point of view that it does not matter what is painted as long as it is painted well reduces art to craftsmanship, Gottlieb feels.

A new subject matter is coming into being. It comes through free association and automatism used as a direct way of "tapping" the unconscious for new ideas. Symbols may appear which resemble primitive art, but primitive art came from the same source. The same symbols may appear at various places and after intervals of many years. Thus a relationship arises which could not depend on the conscious mind. The surrealist painters tried to deal with unconscious symbolism but usually only illustrated

Freud. Gottlieb feels that painting has an autonomous development which may determine what the artist does.

Impressionism depended on a change in subject matter as well as in technique. Even [as] painters began to work out of doors the problem of the subject arose in a new way. Cubism again took the subject back to the studio, and surrealism is again a "new twist" on subject matter. In connection with this, Gottlieb says that the work of the present group of "intra-subjective" painters should not be considered an elimination of the subject but a way of dealing with it that has not been used before. Free association is a way of going to an "inner nature" which may not be visual but which, never-the-less, is a part of experience. Gottlieb comments that when people say "go back to nature," they usually mean "go back."

Painting, to Gottlieb, is not only a matter of colors and shapes on canvas, but images made visible and integrated. It is impossible to detach color, form or subject since experience with pictures depends on the integration of these elements. None of the painters of the intra-subjective group value the object as such, nor do they try to imitate the subject matter of the French. There is an inward looking rather than an outward approach. They are "not necessarily fed up with the spiritual or the material world, but all subject matter referring to these has been used up." Gottlieb believes it is significant that these American artists are exploring advanced ideas in the way the French once were explorers. However the younger French artists seem satisfied to go back to the ideas of their older idols and to incorporate these ideas in pictures that will look good over a fireplace. They believe there are no new frontiers and that it is necessary to go back. The American artists have found new frontiers. Painting is a matter of continually "throwing away excess baggage." The academic artist tries to become rich by accumulating and hoarding. The non-academic artist continually discards. It is necessary not to become too self-critical as this is a neurotic tendency. The only way to be productive is to keep on working and searching for [*illegible*] creative periods. The artist must remember that no one like himself ever existed before and must assert himself, which implies an element of violence. Gottlieb came to think of "decomposition" not as a matter of tearing down art, but of adjusting composition to his own needs. In thinking of their work, artists should consider the artistic issues involved, Gottlieb feels, and think seriously about their subjects. Always there should be the spirit of advancing art.

One characteristic of the artists of this group is the lack of focal point, which was seldom stressed by the French artists. The interest is distributed throughout the surface of the canvas.

To be an explorer in the field of painting may not be easy but Gottlieb says, "If one chooses to be an explorer, he should not complain if he has to eat K rations [*sic*]."

Willem de Kooning

FROM AN INTERVIEW

With de Kooning, the presence or absence of recognizable objects in a painting is not of importance. He admires the work of the old masters and often refers to Velasquez, Michelangelo and Cézanne. However, he points out that many think of the work of those men as "glorified calendar paintings," or merely a professional approach to the handling of recognizable objects. This, de Kooning says, is not the case with these men. The importance of their work does not lie in the imitation of nature but rather in the fact that their subjects are handled in such a way as to present a new experience. Thus the sky in a Corot landscape is not the sky we see in nature but presents an experience belonging typically to Corot. Today it is difficult to react to objects as something to be painted. A tree, for instance, has already been done in so many different ways in the past that de Kooning feels he would not know how to paint it without repeating what has already been done.

During the interview de Kooning pointed to the stove pipe in his studio. "The light on that stovepipe may move a person in the way countless sensations are caused throughout the day," he said, "yet somehow there is the feeling that the light belongs on the stovepipe. If it is transferred to a painting it does not seem as meaningful to me." The oil can beside the stove he referred to as reality but enjoyed seeing it as such and not as something necessary to his painting. A painting should be as real as an oil can, and he thinks of his paintings as being as independent and self-sufficient as the oil can. They must exist without being dependent.

De Kooning is moved by the intenseness of New York, the electric signs, the conglomeration of buildings, and would not want to have this changed. He is not sympathetic with the dictator attitude whereby an architect would rebuild an entire city in his own way. The variation of the aspects of life are what give meaning to the city and reflect the personalities and lives of the many kinds of people who make up the city.

De Kooning does not paint from a sense of social responsibility. He tries to express those values most meaningful to himself and to satisfy himself only. Somewhere, he feels, there will be those who will react to his paintings, but he must not be concerned with this. The many problems of his own that he must face as an artist are given first consideration. And to those who bemoan the situation of the artist today he answers that he finds the artist to be in a fortunate position. There is no one to limit his freedom since few understand the frontiers where he walks. No one should ask the artist to conform. That is not his job. Even if he were to conform, what would he conform to? Certainly in the world today it would be difficult to know where and how to adjust.

It is noteworthy that today painting is often biographical. De Kooning referred to Géricault who at an early age painted the "Raft of the Medusa" which was soon accepted as an important painting. Now the one-man show becomes a history of the artist's states of being, the individual picture is often considered only as related to other works and the question at an artist's show is, "What change will he go through next?" Pictures are not usually accepted on their own merit.

The time of the great innovators has passed. Picasso and Matisse have done their work and have become heroes. De Kooning does not think of himself as an innovator, or of innovation as valid today. "This is the end of a period in painting," he says, "but within this period are the beginnings of a new one."

ANALYSIS

The statement by de Kooning that the presence or absence of recognizable objects is not of importance in painting implies that subject matter may actually not be concerned primarily with objects or representation.

De Kooning shows that he feels the [*unclear, concealed by sticker*] a painting does not depend on representing what already. . . .[8]

8. This analysis appears to be incomplete.

Part III

Results of the Research

SUMMARY

The following points are derived from the interviews and analyses of the interviews and are presented to show the attitudes of the intrasubjectivists in terms of the problem of subject matter in painting, and on the development of arts.

The presence or absence of recognizable forms in painting is irrelevant to its validity.

While these artists deal with forms that do not come from existing objects, or work with subjective symbols that may suggest objects, they at the same time, believe that art is not limited to any one means of expression.

They feel that today, however, the most valid painting comes from a different source than painting of the past. So much painting has been done by looking at models and landscapes that those subjects offer nothing new to work with.

By turning to the subconscious a vast, new field is opened up in which exploration is possible, and, though there may at times be the hesitance and look of sureness that any explorer feels, the discovery of a new source from which to derive subject will add life blood to art.

The artists feel that the center of art interest is shifting from Paris to this country, yet as this happens the work will be characterized by universal, rather than nationalistic, subject matter. The shifting is taking place because of new sources of painting material which American artists seem to be more conscious of.

Though these artists turn to the same source for subjects, they stress individuality and believe there is as wide a range of subjects as there are personalities involved.

Some of the artists are concerned with symbols coming from the subconscious that, at times, may resemble existing objects and become meaningful through association. Others wish to eliminate all associational experience.

Most of the artists interviewed feel that the term "intrasubjectivists" is only a term of identification and not necessarily an adequate descriptive term. It stress[es] the fact that they are a group whereas the merit of the artists as individuals is what will, in the long run, determine the value of what is being done.

CONCLUSIONS

The intrasubjectivist creates from an internal world rather than an external one. At the same time there is an increasingly older range of subject matter depending on the personalities of the artists.

Painting seems to depend less and less on expressive means of the past. A new subject matter and a new approach to its source has come about, resulting in a new vitality in painting.

Another quotation from Ortega states the position of contemporary painting.

> The guiding law of the great variations in painting is one of disturbing simplicity. First, things are painted; then sensations, finally, ideas. This means that in the beginning the artist's attention was fixed on external reality; then on the subjective, finally on the intrasubjective. These three stages are three points on a straight line. . . . After Cezanne, painting only paints ideas—which, certainly, are objects also, but ideal objects, immanent to subject or intrasubjective.[9]

9. José Ortega y Gasset, "On Point of View of the Arts," *Partisian Review* 8 (August 1949): 834.

Finally, the question of the presence or absence of recognizable forms as part of the content of painting is an irrelevant question.

DISCUSSION

The writer feels that the clarification of attitudes toward subject matter and its source, as expressed through these interviews, may be of assistance to art teachers as well as to students who are in the process of finding their own position. The changes taking place in the art world should be known to students so that they may form a clear idea of what is involved, whether or not the students agree as to the validity of the issues. It is felt that art teachers should bring the intrasubjectivists to the attention of students, if only because of the acceptance of those artists by leading museums and galleries throughout this country and abroad. In classes where abstract painting is taught, students often need to be shown why they are working in that way so that they do not merely think it is the "thing to do."

Because of growing interest in the source of subject matter and in working with subjects derived through the subconscious, the number of artists working in this way is increasing. Since so little is known about subconscious processes, it is probable that further research, including ideas of many younger artists now forming their points of view, will bring to light valuable material in regards to these processes. Research from a psychological point of view should be of help both to the arts and to psychology. Research through analization [*sic*] of the paintings of these men and of material written on the subject matter of the artist should add to an awareness of the value of art in our time. If such work can be done while the movement is going on, material may be available that can never be found once the movement becomes history.

Mondrian describes this epoch as difficult but interesting. He says, "After a secular culture, a turning point has arrived; this shows itself in all the branches of human activity... in art some have discovered the artistic laws relating to plastics. In spite of all opposition, these facts have become movements."[10]

10. Piet Mondrian, *Plastic Art and Pure Plastic Art and Other Essays* (New York: Wittenborn, Schultz, Inc., 1947): 53.

"Pollock paints a picture"

ARTnews 50, no. 3 (May 1951): 38–41, 60–61.

E.N.: *When the article originally appeared, the credit, "Photographs by Hans Nemuth [Namuth]" appeared alongside the title.*

Far out on Long Island, in the tiny village of Springs, with the ocean as background and in close contact with open, tree-studded fields where cattle graze peacefully, Jackson Pollock lives and paints. With the help of his wife, Lee Krasner—former Hofmann student and an established painter in her own right—he has remodeled a house purchased there to fit the needs of the way of life they have chosen, and a short distance away is a barn which has been converted into a studio. It is here that Pollock is engrossed in the strenuous job of creating his unique world as a painter.

Before settling on the Island, Pollock worked for ten years in a Greenwich Village studio. Intermittently he made trips across the country, riding freight trains or driving a Model A Ford, developing a keen awareness of vast landscape and open sky. "You get a wonderful view of the country from the top of a freight car," he explains. Pollock loves the outdoors and has carried with him and into his painting a sense of the freedom experienced before endless mountains and plains, and perhaps this is not surprising in an artist born in Cody, Wyoming (in 1912) and raised in Arizona and northern California. Included in his background is study with Thomas Benton—for whom he was at one time a baby sitter on New York's Hudson Street—but he has mainly developed by himself, in contemplation of the lonesome silence of the open, emerging in the last few years as the most publicized and controversial of the younger abstractionists. He is also one of the most successful.

To enter Pollock's studio is to enter another world, a place where the intensity of the artist's mind and feelings are given full play. It is the unusual quality of this mind, penetrating nature to the core yet never striving to show its surface that has been projected into paintings which captivate many and agitate others by their strange, often violent, ways of expression. At one end of the barn the floor is literally covered with large cans of enamel, aluminum and tube colors—the boards that do show are covered with paint drippings. Nearby a skull rests on a chest of drawers. Three or four cans contain stubby paint brushes of various sizes. About the rest of the studio, on the floor and walls, are paintings in various stages of completion, many of enormous proportions. Here Pollock often sits for hours in deep contemplation of work in progress, his face forming rigid lines and often settling in a heavy frown. A Pollock painting is not born easily, but comes into being after weeks, often months of work and thought. At times he paints with feverish activity, or again with slow deliberation.

After some years of preparation and experimentation, during which time he painted his pictures on an easel, Pollock has developed a method that is unique and that, because of its newness, shocks many. He has found that what he has to say is best accomplished by laying the canvas on the floor, walking around it and applying the paint from all sides. The paint—usually enamel, which he finds more pliable—is applied by dipping a small house brush or stick or trowel into the can and then, by rapid movements of the wrist, arm and body, quickly allowing it to fall in weaving rhythms over the surface. The brush seldom touches the canvas, but is a means to let color drip or run in stringy forms that allow for the complexity of design necessary to the artist.

In his recent show, at the Parsons Gallery, Pollock exhibited a very large work, titled *Number 4, 1950.* (Pollock used to give his pictures conventionally symbolic titles, but—like many contemporary abstractionists—he considers them misleading, and now simply numbers and dates each work as it is completed.) It was begun on a sunny day last June. The canvas, 9 by 17 feet, was laid out flat, occupying most of the floor of the studio and Pollock stood gazing at it for some time, puffing at a cigarette. After a while he took a can of black enamel (he usually starts with the color which is at hand at the time) and a stubby brush which he dipped into the paint and then began to move his arm rhythmically about, letting the paint fall in a variety of movement on the surface. At times he would crouch, holding the brush close to the canvas, and again he would stand and move around it or step on it to reach to the middle. Within a half hour the entire surface had taken on an activity of weaving rhythms. Pools of black, tiny streams and elongated forms seemed to become transformed and began to take on the appearance of an image. As he continued, still with black, going back over former areas, rhythms were intensified with counteracting movements. After some time he decided to stop to consider what had been done. This might be called the first step of the painting, though Pollock stresses that he does not work in stages. He did not know yet when he would feel strongly enough about the picture to work on it again, with the intensity needed, nor when he would finally be finished with it. The paint was allowed to dry, and the next day it was nailed to a wall of the studio for a period of study and concentration.

It was about two weeks before Pollock felt close enough to the work to go ahead again This was a time of "getting acquainted" with the painting, of thinking about it and getting used to it so that he might tell what needed to be done to increase its strength. The feverish intensity of the actual painting process could not be kept up indefinitely, but long periods of contemplation and thought must aid in the preparation for renewed work. In the meantime other paintings were started. When he felt able to return to the large canvas with renewed energy, Pollock placed it back on the floor, selected a light reddish brown color and began again to work in rhythms and drops that fell on uncovered areas of canvas and over the black. Occasionally aluminum paint was added, tending to hold the other colors on the same plane as the canvas. (Pollock uses metallic paint much in the same sense that earlier painters applied gold leaf, to add a feeling of mystery and adornment to the work and to keep it from being thought of as occupying the accepted world of things. He finds that aluminum often accomplishes this more successfully than greys, which he first used.) Again the painting was allowed to dry and then hung on the wall for a few days' renewed consideration.

The final work on the painting was slow and deliberate. The design had become exceedingly complex and had to be brought to a state of complete organization. When finished and free from himself the painting would record a released experience. A few movements in white paint constituted the final act and the picture was hung on the wall; then the artist decided there was nothing more he could do with it.

Pollock felt that the work had become "concrete"—he says that he works "from the abstract to the concrete," rather than vice versa: the painting does not depend on reference to any object or tactile surface, but exists "on its own." Pollock feels that criticism of a work such as this should be directed at least in terms of what he is doing, rather than by standards of what painting ought to be. He is aware that a new way of expression in art is often difficult to see, but he resents presentation of his work merely on the level of technical interest.

Such a summation of Pollock's way of working is, of course, only part of the story. It has developed after years of concentrated effort, during long periods when nothing was satisfactory to him. He explains that he spent four years painting "black pictures," pictures which were unsuccessful. Then his work began to be more sure. There was a period of painting symbols, usually of figures or monsters, violently expressed. Of them, She Wolf [*sic*], now owned by the Museum of Modern Art, was a crucial work. Here areas of brush-work and paint-pouring were combined, the painting being done partly on the floor and partly on the easel. The change to his way of working today was gradual, accompanying his various needs for expression, and though there is a sense of the brutal in what he does this gradually seems to be giving way to greater calm.

During the cataclysmic upheavals painting has undergone in recent years there have been rather drastic measures taken with the object. It has been distorted and finally eliminated as a reference point by many artists. The questions arise as to what the artist is dealing with, where he gets his ideas, what his subject matter is, etc. The answer may be found partly in the consideration that these artists are not concerned with representing a preconceived idea, but rather with being involved in an experience of paint and canvas, directly, without interference from the suggested forms and colors of existing objects. The nature of the experience is important. It is not something that has lost contact with reality, but might be called a synthesis of countless contacts which have become refined in the area of the emotions during the act of painting. Is this merely an act of automatism? Pollock says it is not. He feels that his methods may be automatic at the start, but that they quickly step beyond that, becoming concerned with deeper and more involved emotions which carry the painting on to completion according to their degree of strength and purity. He does not know beforehand how a work of his will end. He is impelled to work by the urge to create and this urge and what it produces are forever unknowable. We see paint on a canvas, but the beauty to which we respond is of an intangible order. We can experience the unknowable, but not understand it intellectually.

Pollock depends on the intensity of the moment of starting to paint to determine the release of his emotions and the direction the picture will take. No sketches are used. Decisions about the painting are made during its development and it is considered completed when he no longer feels any affinity with it.

The work of art may be called an image which is set between the artist and the spectator. A Pollock reveals his personal way of bringing this image into existence. Starting automatically, almost as a ritual dance might begin, the graceful rhythms of his movements seem to determine to a large extent the way the paint is applied, but underlying this is the complex Pollock mind. At first he is very much alone with a picture, forgetting that there is a world of people and activity outside himself. Gradually, he again becomes aware of the outside world and the image he has begun to project is thought of as related to both himself and other people. He is working toward something objective, something which in the end may exist independently of himself, and that may be presented directly to others. His work may be thought of as coming from landscape and even the movement of the stars—with which he seems almost intimate at times—yet it does not depend on representing these, but rather on creating an image as resulting from contemplation of a complex universe at work, as though to make his own world of reality and order. He is involved in the world of art, the area in which man undertakes to express his finest feelings, which, it seems, is best done through love. Pollock, a quiet man who speaks with reserve and to the point, is in love with his work and his whole life evolves [*sic*] about what he is doing.

He feels that his most successful paintings carry the same intensity directly to the edges of the canvas. "My paintings do not have a center," he says, "but depend on the same amount of interest throughout." Since it has no reference to objects that exist, or to ideal objects, such as circles and squares, his work must be considered from the point of view of expression through the integration of rhythm, color and design, which he feels beauty is composed of. Physical space is dispensed with as an element in painting—even the dimensions of the canvas do not represent measurements inside which relationships are set up, but rather only determine the ends of the image.

Pollock's *Number 4, 1950*[1] is concerned with creating an image in these terms. In this it is like much of his other work, but it is also among his most successful paintings, its manifold tensions and rhythms balancing and counteracting each other so that the final state is one of rest: movements have not been resolved. Colors in *Number 4, 1950* have been applied so that one is not concerned with them as separate areas: the browns, blacks, silver and white move within one another to achieve an integrated whole in which one is aware of color rather than colors. Nor is the concern with space here. There is no feeling that one might walk bodily into the rectangle and move about. This is irrelevant, the pleasure being of a different nature. It is more

---

1. The article includes a confusing anomaly that contradicts Goodnough's description of Pollock's painting process, specifically his use of aluminum (silver) paint. The painting illustrated and identified in the text as *Number 4, 1950* (now known as *Autumn Rhythm: Number 30, 1950,* Metropolitan Museum of Art, New York), contains no aluminum paint. In all other respects, Goodnough's account is accurate—the canvas measures roughly 9 by 17 feet, and is composed of layers of black, brown, and white paint applied in the manner described. Hans Namuth's photographs illustrating the article show Pollock at work on *Autumn Rhythm,* but the images are black and white, so the lack of silver is not apparent. It may be that since, by his own later admission, Goodnough did not actually watch Pollock paint it, he confused it with one of the other canvases in the Betty Parsons Gallery exhibition in November–December 1950, in which *Autumn Rhythm* was included. The painting now titled *Number 4, 1950* (Carnegie Museum of Art, Pittsburgh) was also in that exhibition and does contain aluminum paint, as well as several other colors, but the canvas is only 49 by 38 inches. Contrary to Goodnough's statement that Pollock "numbers and dates each work as it is completed," the numerical system is not chronological. We know from Namuth's photographs that *Number 32, 1950* (Kunstsammlung Nordrhein-Westfalen, Düsseldorf) was completed before *Number 31, 1950* (Museum of Modern Art, New York), which was finished before *Autumn Rhythm: Number 30, 1950* was begun.

of an emotional experience from which the physical has been removed, and to this intangible quality we sometimes apply the word "spiritual."

In this picture Pollock has almost completely eliminated everything that might interfere with enjoyment of his work on this level. It is true that painting is seen through the senses, but they are only a means for conveying the image to the aesthetic mind. One is not earthbound in looking at *Number 4, 1950;* in lesser paintings one does not feel this sense of release from physical reactions. The experience Pollock himself has had with this high kind of feeling is what gives quality to his work. Of course anyone can pour paint on a canvas, as anyone can bang on a piano, but to create one must purify the emotions; few have the strength, will or even the need to do this.

"Statement"

It is 1 (Spring 1958): 46.

I first studied painting in an academic way from copying models and casts, and learning to paint portraits. But the domination of the object looked at, always saying that a certain line should go in this direction or that, a red had to be here and a blue there because that was the way it was on the model, began to be limiting. What does yellow mean? I felt that the painting would compose better if there were some red down in the right corner, yet according to the model there should be a hand there which could not be red. The composition, it seemed, should not be unalterably determined by what one was looking at and attempting to paint. Composing, or building colors and relationships of shapes on a canvas, became more important in itself. Gradually the subject, a group of figures or a street scene, was ignored or taken apart, and the shapes rearranged to form a more stable design and the subject itself might disappear or emerge in a new way. Or a painting might be started without a particular subject in mind, and a relationship of shapes might suggest an idea. This idea could be abstract (or without recognizable objects) or it could develop into recognizable things. A great deal of freedom was then possible at the outset of the painting. The necessary discipline and decision could come about as the picture developed.

Something of this kind has apparently happened with many abstract painters today—a need for release from imposed conventions and from "ways of doing it" that have registered within the painter from experiences with pictures since childhood. There seems to be a development from the tactile (in which things are represented to look almost as though one could reach out and touch them) to a more purely visual expression, where one experiences the painting in itself unrelated to outside experiences. This turning away from the object, or the tactile, seems to characterize a contemporary tendency of thought as well as of artistic expression. Pure mathematics becomes important in itself; the importance of pure research is stressed. There is dissatisfaction with the over concern with objects as possessions.

There is a feeling in the best work of American painters of the "wild" which has been the heritage of this country. The covered wagons, the Indians, the rolling prairies, the immense forests and mountains are part of one's memory. Thoreau's belief that dullness and tameness are the same, that it is the wild that attracts us in literature, seems also to apply to painting. There is something of the surprise element in a work of art. It leads one to think, perhaps, in a way one has not thought before.

Biographical Summary

Robert Arthur Goodnough was born in the small town of Cortland, in the Finger Lakes region of upstate New York, on October 23, 1917. After earning his bachelor's degree in fine arts from Syracuse University in 1940, he was drafted into the United States Army and served in the field artillery during World War II. While stationed in New Guinea he became aware of modern art by reading magazines—his training at Syracuse had been strictly conservative. As he told the author and art collector B. H. Friedman, "I was tired of painting people that looked like people, with eyes, nose and mouth in just the right places." [1] He decided, "To make some changes and free up a bit. It seemed that in order to grasp the true energy of a person more was needed than to show features, arms and legs. People moved and did things; they didn't just sit and pose; and what they did came from underlying energies and drives." [2]

In 1946, following his discharge from the service, Goodnough moved to New York City and attended the Amédée Ozenfant School of Fine Arts under the G.I. Bill. He also studied at Hans Hofmann's summer school in Provincetown, Massachusetts, and began to meet members of the New York art world, including the critic Clement Greenberg. Together with fellow Hoffman students, Larry Rivers and Alfred Leslie,

---

1. Barbara Guest and B. H. Friedman, *goodnough* (Paris: Editions Georges Fall/The Pocket Museum, 1962): 12.
2. Ibid.

he earned a master's degree in art from New York University in 1950, after which he taught at the Fieldston School in the Bronx, and later at Cornell University. His work exploited the tension produced by explosive energy held in check by a solid structural framework. As he explained, "I like to work freely, to slash with the brush and let loose. I also like to work carefully and with discipline." His study with Ozenfant, a founder of Purism, and Hofmann, a proponent of Cubism, combined with his admiration of Abstract Expressionism's freedom and vitality, created this dynamic ambiguity.

Goodnough credited the architect and sculptor Tony Smith with opening the door to the New York avant garde. "Smith showed me around, so to speak," he later wrote, "and he introduced me to several artists who were just emerging as prominent players on the new art scene."[3] His association with Studio 35 and the Club helped him overcome the feeling that he was an outsider in the tight-knit urban vanguard. On Elaine de Kooning's recommendation, he wrote art reviews and feature articles for *ARTnews* from 1950 to 1957. In addition to his now-famous article on Pollock, he also wrote on Franz Kline and the sculptors David Hare, Saul Baizerman, and Herbert Ferber in the magazine's series on visits to artists' studios.

His first one-person exhibition was held at the Wittenborn Gallery in 1950, the same year that his work was featured in the *New Talent* show, selected by Greenberg and the art historian Meyer Schapiro, at the Kootz Gallery. The following year he was included in the 9th Street Show, and he exhibited regularly in the Stable Gallery and Whitney Museum annuals throughout the 1950s and '60s. He was represented from 1952–70 and 1984–86 by the Tibor de Nagy Gallery; in the 1970s and '80s by the André Emmerich Gallery in Manhattan and the Harcus Krakow

3. "Goodnough Paints a Word Picture: Recollections of Pollock and the New York School," in *Goodnough paints a picture,* exhibition brochure, Pollock-Krasner House and Study Center, 2002, n.p.

Gallery in Boston. Solo exhibitions of his work were held at the Art Institute of Chicago (1960 and '61); the Whitney Museum of American Art, New York, and the Albright-Knox Art Gallery, Buffalo (1969); and the Neuberger Museum of Art, Purchase, New York (1999). A traveling solo exhibition went to venues in the United States and London in 1964.

Goodnough's work has been included in numerous group exhibitions, including the traveling exhibitions *Nature in Abstraction*, circulated by the Whitney (1958), *The Art of Assemblage*, circulated by the Museum of Modern Art (1961–62), and MoMA's *Hans Hofmann and His Students* (1963–64), as well as the 1970 Venice Biennale. It is in the collections of major museums throughout the country, including MoMA; the Whitney; the Neuberger; the Metropolitan Museum of Art; the Solomon R. Guggenheim Museum; the Museum of Fine Arts, Boston; the Smithsonian American Art Museum; the San Diego Museum of Art; the Art Institute of Chicago; the Portland Art Museum; the Chrysler Museum; the Albright-Knox; and the Memorial Art Gallery, University of Rochester, as well as many private collections. His public art is in the Empire State Plaza Art Collection in Albany, New York; the Manufacturers Hanover Trust Building in Manhattan; the New Castle County Courthouse in Wilmington, Delaware; Chappaqua Library in Chappaqua, New York; and the Ossining, New York Metro North station, among other locations.

A lifelong woodworker, Goodnough turned to sculpture in the 1980s, while continuing to paint and create collages. Solo exhibitions of his recent paintings were presented at the Katharina Rich Perlow Gallery in Manhattan in 2005, and at the Margot Stein Gallery, Lake Worth, Florida, in 2008. At the time of his death on October 2, 2010, he was living in Thornwood, New York.

HAH

Subject Matter of the Artist:
Writings by Robert Goodnough, 1950–1965

"AS A PAINTER and as one interested in education in relation to painting and drawing, the writer has become personally interested in the problem of subject matter in art.... Since there is controversy in regards to this tendency in painting, research directed toward the source of ideas involved in the work, it is felt, will help to make clear the intention of the artists. This research will deal with the attitudes of these artists toward their own work and their relation to tradition as they express it." —Robert Goodnough (1950)

THE ABSENCE OF TRADITIONAL subject matter was a primary issue for painters in mid-twentieth-century America whose imagery lacked representational references; it was also a problem for those struggling to understand modern art. Robert Goodnough (1917–2011), then a New York University graduate student and an artist deeply involved with these issues, responded to the situation in a 1950 research paper, "Subject Matter of the Artist: An Analysis of Contemporary Subject Matter in Painting as Derived from Interviews with Those Artists Referred to as the Intrasubjectivists." Goodnough's paper constitutes the first scholarly work on the artists who became known as the Abstract Expressionists and includes interviews with William Baziotes, Willem de Kooning, Adolph Gottlieb, Robert Motherwell, Barnett Newman, Jackson Pollock, and Mark Rothko. This previously unpublished study is presented here for the first time alongside related writings by Goodnough.

HELEN A. HARRISON is an art historian, journalist, and Director of the Pollock-Krasner House and Study Center in East Hampton, NY.

IRVING SANDLER is an art critic, curator, and Professor Emeritus of Visual Arts at SUNY-Purchase.